# Small Wonder

## Squaw Island
### Canandaigua Lake

Preston E. Pierce

Ontario County Historical Society
Canandaigua, New York

ISBN 0-941198-10-3

© Preston E. Pierce
2003

# Table of Contents

Small Wonder: Squaw Island, Canandaigua Lake ............................................................... 1

A Legendary Place ............................................................................................................ 2

Nineteenth Century Backwater ....................................................................................... 4

"Water Biscuits" ................................................................................................................. 7

Gifts of Mary Clark Thompson .......................................................................................... 9

Hard Times Befall the Island ............................................................................................ 11

Local Preservation Efforts Begin ..................................................................................... 13

Squaw Island Preservation Society ................................................................................. 15

John M. Clarke and the "Water Biscuits" of Squaw Island ............................................ 21

"The Water Biscuit of Squaw Island" (1900 reprint) ....................................................... 23

Charles T. Mitchell: Physician, Angler and Writer .......................................................... 28

"A Romance of Squaw Island" (1915 reprint) ................................................................ 29

Notes ................................................................................................................................ 33

# DEDICATION

Granger Green                    Paul Hudson                    Clifford Murphy, Sr.

Squaw Island has held a special place in the hearts of generations. It has been a source of pleasure, relaxation, and inspiration. The island has provided a pleasant place to fish, swim, and have a picnic. A reminder of our Native-American heritage, the island has provided scientists and laypeople with insight into the workings of nature.

While the island has often been neglected and taken for granted, it has been a source of pride, and a focus of curiosity, for tens of thousands. It has had many friends. For nearly a century, however, four men focused attention on Squaw Island, elevated its status, and kept the faith in the righteous cause of preserving its soft shores. More than any others, they deserve the credit for the continued interest in the island and its preservation.

Dr. John Mason Clarke, Granger Green, and Clifford Murphy, Sr. have all "crossed over the bar." This story of the verdant bar they loved is dedicated to them. Paul Hudson, founder of the Squaw Island Preservation Society, was largely responsible for the valiant effort which ensured the preservation of the island. He focused the dedicated efforts of many others and now shares in this dedication.

# Small Wonder:
# Squaw Island, Canandaigua Lake

At one time or another, we have all gazed beyond the Canandaigua city pier and considered it. Some of us have seen it from a quiet sailboat, or even beached our boats in the soft gravel off its shore. Tour boats cruise by it several times each day. Few of us ever realize, however, the significance of this small wonder lying beside our busiest channel.

The island has beckoned those who live in this "chosen spot;" even for a brief visit. They have seen it as they wanted to see it. A little more than a century ago, local artists, like Charles Wader, Fred Crandall, and Edward G. Hayes brought the allure of Squaw Island into parlors throughout the region.[1] Their example has been followed by a succession of modern painters and photographers. Now, however, with the word "squaw" in ill repute, we aren't even sure what we should call this small wonder in Canandaigua Lake.[2]

Edward G. Hayes. *Circa* 1895. Courtesy Mrs. Dorothy Maffin.

# A Legendary Place

Squaw Island takes it name from a story which has been passed down since at least 1861.[3] In the late 1800's, when there was renewed interest in our early history, some notes appeared in a local paper stating that Native-American women had taken refuge on Squaw Island during the Sullivan Expedition in 1779. No one knows when the public first became aware of the story. Most likely, it is a reflection of the romantic 19th Century view of the tragic "noble savage." Such stories endure, however. In 1915 Dr. Charles T. Mitchell of Canandaigua wrote a lengthy poem, "A Romance of Squaw Island," which was widely distributed. The esteemed scientist and director of the State Museum, Dr. John M. Clarke, summed up the prevailing view in a comment published in a local paper. "If Squaw Island did not have an Indian legend, it certainly ought to have one..."[4]

There was a Seneca-Iroquois village about a mile from the island in 1779. It was probably located near the present Thompson Hospital.[5] Along the lake, settlers later found evidence that Native-Americans used the northern lake shore as a work site. A carved rock, now on the lawn of the Ontario County Historical Society museum, was found along the east shore of the lake near the present City of Canandaigua.[6] It was probably used for shaping arrow points and other objects. At the west end of Kershaw Park a plaque was placed on a stone monument in 1919. It marks the site where 16 Native-Americans were re-interred after their graves were disturbed on the nearby Garrat farm during the construction of the old Swimming School in 1905-06. Other small sites have been found around the City of Canandaigua. However, no clear evidence can be found to positively identify the site of the historical native village.

Seneca-Iroquois society had clearly defined roles for men and women. Women chose the governmental leaders, ran the families, and performed village and field tasks. They would have had little use for the island except for recreation. It is highly unlikely that the respected women of the village attempted to hide on the island, as large as it was in 1779. More likely, they retreated to the forest, or took refuge in one of the nearby fishing and hunting camps like the one on Seneca Point.

General John Sullivan's 5000-man detachment of the Continental army marched through the Finger Lakes in 1779. Their mission was the destruction of the homes and crops of the Iroquois nations that had allied themselves with Britain. They burned crops, destroyed villages, and cut down fruit trees. Many of the soldiers marveled at the productive land they saw. Several dozen kept journals of the expedition which have been collected and published. On September 8, 1779 General Sullivan's forces entered the Seneca village at Canandaigua. Some of the journals say more than others. None of them mention the island, but several detail the activity of the army around Canandaigua.[7] Dr. Jabez Campfield, Surgeon in the 5th New Jersey Regiment, told of riding "into the lake about 10 rod and found it about 2 feet or 18 inches deep and believe it mostly that depth, having a white sandy bottom and the water very clear." Others made similar entries. Lieutenant Benjamin Lodge, surveyor of the expedition, did not show the island on the map he produced. The island was obviously not a concern to Sullivan's troopers.[8] Had there been reason to believe potential captives were on the island, the experienced frontier fighters with Sullivan, including a detachment of the legendary Morgan Riflemen, would surely have investigated. It is hard to believe the native inhabitants would have been foolish enough to hide on an island so easily cut off and in shallow water.

The island looking north *circa* 1900. It probably looked much like this in 1779.

# Nineteenth Century Backwater

Throughout the Nineteenth Century, Squaw Island was literally in a quiet backwater of the lake. Diaries, journals, and local reminiscences speak of the island as a good place to fish, or a quiet, perhaps romantic, spot to row. In the era when bathtubs and running water were luxuries, Squaw Island also provided "a capital place for soiled humanity to have a good cheap bath out of sight and hearing," according to one reader of the *Ontario County Journal*.[9]

At the turn of the Twentieth Century, the importance of Squaw Island mostly rested upon its scenic beauty, making it a fit subject for the newly invented picture postcard, and the island's growing identification with Native-American women. It served little other purpose beyond just being available.

By 1875, Squaw Island was also the source of a great deal of local construction gravel. That year, a lengthy letter to the editor of the *Ontario County Journal* set forth specific complaints.

> "Already gravel enough has been taken away on the west side to make a trench that is about four rods long, twelve feet wide, and four feet deep, and thereby undermining three or four large trees which, after high water, will be no more. On the east side about the same amount has been dug out toward the centre and taken away, about three or four hundred loads altogether. Part of this amount has been taken to improve the lake shore road..."[10]

The problem apparently continued for some years. In 1881, The *Ontario County Times* noted the efforts to curb abuse of the island.

> "The authorities of this village have caused a notice to be placed on 'Squaw Island' in Canandaigua Lake, forbidding all persons from taking or removing there from any sand or gravel. This is eminently proper; but a similar step should have been taken years ago, as the island has been gradually disappearing and reappearing again on the premises of 'private citizens.'"[11]

By late summer, and into the fall and winter, it was possible to reach the island without getting your feet wet. Sometimes cattle grazed there. The phenomenon was often noted in the local papers. In November, 1895, the *Times* told its readers,

> "The lake continues to fall, and a broader extent of beach is not uncovered than any one living has ever before seen. One may walk dry shod from the shore to Squaw Island."[12]

Just four years later, the *Journal* described how the low lake level was affecting the island once again.

> "The level of the lake has lowered perceptibly during the past week. The island is no longer an island, but the end of a peninsula. The flag (weeds) has attained an immense growth in the cove west of the pier, and, holding about its roots decaying animal and vegetable matter, emits an unhealthful and disease-ladened stench."[13]

In September, 1903, the *Journal* reported that,

> "the lake is low enough to expose the sand bar most of the distance from the shore to the island, almost making a peninsula of the latter."[14]

Three years later that same paper said,

> "The lake level remains low and the island is now a peninsula. The ribs of an old sailing barge which sank west of the pier so many years ago that few of the present generation recall it, are now visible."[15]

The established steamboat routes bypassed Squaw Island. In 1827, the first steamboat on the lake, the *Lady of the Lake*, was launched just west of the island.[16] Several more, like the *Onnalinda*, were built along city pier and plied the water past Squaw Island. Ice was harvested around the island while the Brady and McCormick ice houses were in business.

In 1884 the Village of Canandaigua granted a franchise for a private pumping station on Main Street near the present state boat launching site. The company laid water mains on the principal streets of Canandaigua and put a 2500 foot intake pipe into the lake south and east of Squaw Island (across the present boat channel). The "crib" built around the old intake was not removed until 1903. That year, a dredging crew succeeded in removing the old structure. It "disturbed so many boatmen's dreams and so nearly caused many shipwrecks," according to the *Ontario Repository*.[17] The new pumping station on the West Lake Road opened in 1895 putting the private franchise out of business.

By 1903 there were many Italian immigrants working in Canandaigua. Many of them came to work on Mrs. Thompson's Sonnenberg estate. Others came to work for the contractors paving Canandaigua streets with brick. While a few families became permanent residents, many of the immigrant laborers were temporary. There was friction among the workers and with established local residents. By the first decade of the 20th Century local newspapers were publishing sensational stories of crimes committed by immigrants. The editor of the *Ontario County Journal* actually suggested, perhaps with tongue in cheek, that the temporary Italian residents be "colonized" on Squaw Island! [18]

The island from the north end looking south. Postcard dated 1908.

# "Water Biscuits"

By 1918, Squaw Island was important for another reason. Dr. John Mason Clarke, son of legendary Canandaigua Academy Principal, Noah T. Clarke, had identified a peculiar, but significant, lime-carbonate formation there. Initially called "water biscuits," the formations are better known today as *"oncolites."* The Clarkes, cousins of Mary Clark Thompson (of Sonnenberg), were a distinguished family of scholars. Dr. Clarke, who grew up in Canandaigua, was undoubtedly familiar with Squaw Island. By then he was State Paleontologist and Director of the State Museum. He wrote hundreds of articles on the relatively new sciences. In 1918 Clarke proposed making Squaw Island a State Museum Reservation because of its scientific importance. He had written an article on the island and its *oncolites* for the *State Museum Bulletin* in 1900.[19]

The *oncolites* Dr. Clarke described cover the lake bottom around Squaw Island. Later studies confirm that the Squaw Island-type *oncolites* are found only a few places on earth. Unlike those found in north-central New York, Russia, and a few other places, they are all quite small here. Rock-like when picked from the lake, they may soften and disintegrate when dried. Dr. Clarke identified the Sucker Brook watershed as the source of the lime-carbonate for the *oncolites*. The brook feeds the lake after taking a circuitous route flowing north through the Town of Canandaigua, then east, then south. In several places the limestone and calcerous rocks surrounding the brook can be easily identified. The *oncolites* form through the precipitation of calcium-carbonate which hardens around small filaments of algal matter. Modern studies of the phenomenon use the term "Squaw Island" as a type name.[20]

Sucker Brook flows into Canandaigua Lake just north of Squaw Island. Apparently, it is the current from the brook, the action of the waves on the lake, pier and other construction, and the changing depth of the water which formed and reformed the sand bar around the island. The island is, in fact, only a part of the sand bar which is high enough to support vegetation. More important, it is the lime, the currents, and the vegetation which cause the formation of oncolites. Dredging in the area, changes in the Sucker Brook watershed, and the creation of a state boat launching site, appear to have had no effect on the *oncolite* formation, although they have drastically altered the island itself.[21]

View of the island and sandbar, late summer, about 1910. Looking south. Ontario County Historical Society photographic collection.

View of the island from the West Lake Rd about 1940. Notice that cottages are starting to appear on the west shore opposite the island.

# Gifts of Mary Clark Thompson

Mary Clark Thompson encouraged Dr. Clarke's work on Squaw Island, as well as other endeavors of the State Museum. She took a sincere interest in natural science. In 1915 she gave $15,000 to the State Museum for six Iroquois life scenes and $40,000 to rebuild the Williams College chemistry laboratory. In 1919 she gave $10,000 to the National Academy of Science, of which Dr. Clarke was chairman of the geological section, for its geology and paleontology award fund. In her will, Mrs. Thompson left $50,000 to what is now known as the Bronx Zoo. The Clark Reservation south of Syracuse, now part of our state park system, was Mrs. Thompson's gift to the state in honor of her father, Governor Myron H. Clark.[22]

The Canandaigua lakefront held a particular interest for Mrs. Thompson, as well as Dr. Clarke who frequently visited Canandaigua. When a Native-American burial mound was unearthed during the 1905-06 construction of the original Swimming School, Mrs. Thompson erected a monument at their reburial site. She also offered money for lakefront beautification as early as 1911.

While there were several proposals to beautify the pier, the editor of the *Repository and Messenger* promoted the idea of a "Squaw Island Park." That 1904 proposal included using fill from nearby dredging operations to expand and physically preserve the island.[23] Mrs. Thompson and the Rochester and Eastern trolley company independently proposed pier beautification schemes. Later, Mrs. Thompson briefly proposed connecting the island to the pier with decorative bridges. No action was taken on any of those proposals, although some ideas were incorporated into the pier renovations begun in 1909.

In keeping with these interests, Mary Thompson had a huge granite boulder transported to Squaw Island from the Brigham Hall grounds in 1919. Dr. Dwight R. Burrell, donor of the Court House boulder, and chief physician at Brigham Hall, had placed the boulder on the Brigham Hall grounds years before. The boulder, reportedly weighing 10 tons, was transported to Squaw Island by wagon over the sand bar connecting the island to the shore. The work was completed by men from Sonnenberg under the direction of landscape architect and City Engineer, John Handrahan. Mrs. Thompson had a plaque placed on the boulder telling visitors of the significance of the island. The 40 pound plaque disappeared sometime in the 1970s. Clifford Murphy, Sr. located the plaque in a state Department of Transportation office and worked to have it returned to the island. In 1985, two years after Murphy's death, his friends, Granger Green and Leo Hosenfeld, bolted the plaque back on the rock in a short ceremony.

Returning the plaque to the island. Aug. 15, 1985. (Left to right): Dr. Marvin Rapp, former County Historian and executive director of the Chamber of Commerce; Granger Green; Mayor Earl Coleates; Leo Hosenfeld; Ned Holmes, regional supervisor of natural resources, NYS Department of Environmental Conservation. Courtesy Messenger Post Newspapers. *Daily Messenger.* Aug. 15, 1985 (p. 3). Messenger photograph by Tom O'Connor.

# Hard Times Befall the Island

Despite its establishment as a State Museum Reservation, Squaw Island was largely ignored and neglected after 1919. It was a monument, of sorts, to be left alone. Gradually, the island began to disappear. Partly, that was a natural phenomenon, a byproduct of its being a sandbar, as well as its use as a source of gravel. Well before its designation as a State Museum Reservation, Squaw Island was loosing more than its gravel base, however. In May, 1911, the *Ontario County Times* reported,

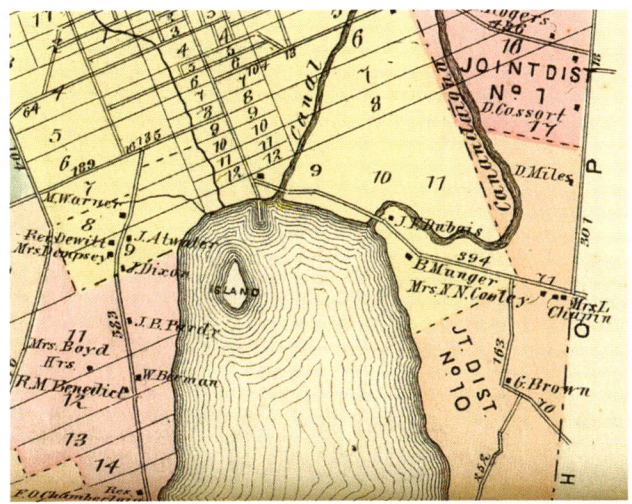

> "The falling of two large elms on Squaw Island gives warning that this historic feature of the lake front will soon be obliterated if steps are not taken for the protection of its shores from wind and waves."[25]

In 1924, City Engineer Handrahan, who had worked closely with Mrs. Thompson for many years, erected a five-foot thick wall of rough stone across the south end of Squaw Island. Handrahan hoped that wall would protect the island from wave and ice erosion. By the mid-20th Century, the diminishing size of the island began to attract the attention of older residents who could remember the island as it was shown in the 1874 county atlas (above).

In later years, Squaw Island "-disappeared" largely because it was being submerged by lake levels higher than nature intended. Two dams controlled by the City of Canandaigua regulate the outlet; one on each channel. The one on the "feeder canal" by Lakeshore Drive is most familiar. The dam in back of the Wegman's supermarket is far enough from Lakeshore Drive and Eastern Boulevard to be relatively unknown. Higher water levels served the boaters who created more waves as boats and their power increased. The wakes of power boats began systematically eating away at the island. The dams prevent the periodic torrents which plagued downstream communities. They remain a permanent and unavoidable threat to the island, particularly during the early spring.

The state paid little attention to the island until it began to look like a financial drain. Jurisdiction over the island was transferred from the State Conservation Commission to the Finger Lakes State Parks Commission in 1928.[26] Aside from providing the basis for the spurious claim that the island was the smallest state park, no other benefit came to the island. Local complaints about the condition of the island prompted state proposals for a dike system encircling the island with concrete in 1949. The State Education Department, which became responsible for the island in 1944, did not carry out the dike construction, however.[27] In 1951 and 1952, the joint state legislative committee on historic sites urged the state to dispose of Squaw Island. Essentially an economy move, the report stated that there were other sources of "water biscuits." It was thought that state money was better spent on improving other sites. The decision met with mild consternation in the Canandaigua area. Little was done. Up to that time, it would appear that the state had spent little, if any, money on Squaw Island.[28]

For a decade the state tried to sell the island which has always been state property. As part of the lake bottom, the island has always been state property by virtue of the decision of the New York State Court of Appeals in *Granger v. City of Canandaigua* (257 NY 126, 1931). It was offered to Ontario County for $1.00. There were no takers.

# Local Preservation Efforts Begin

In 1975 the Canandaigua City Bicentennial Committee proposed a restoration plan for Squaw Island. Based on estimates of the Army Corps of Engineers, the committee sought $50,000-$90,000 in federal, state, and local funding. The success of the plan was doubtful from the start. The project was dropped after it was learned that the island would likely become part of the State Nature and Historical Preserve Trust under pending legislation.[29]

While it was put under the Trust, no money was appropriated for preservation of Squaw Island until two men began a concerted campaign to get state action. In February, 1969, the *Daily Messenger* reported on the private efforts of Clifford E. Murphy, Sr. and Granger Green. For years, the two men wrote letters, lobbied state officials, and even took personal charge of cleaning up the island. It took five years for Murphy, Green, and their friends to secure state funding.[30]

Vandalism and littering were problems on the island at least as far back as 1924. That summer, John Handrahan told the *Times* that he "deplored the use of the (Thompson) boulder as a background for picnic fires," saying that the practice was "the worst sort of vandalism."

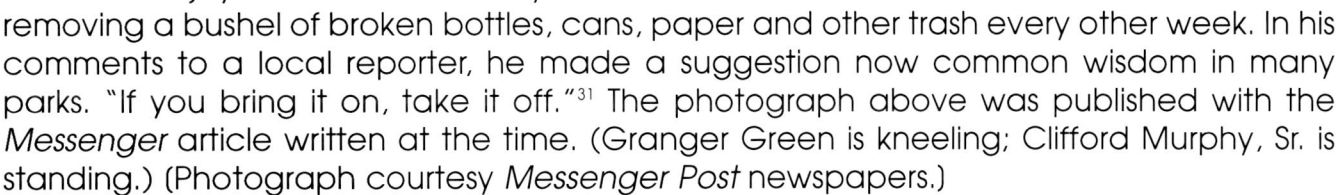

In 1979, Granger Green erected a small sign, "Island to enjoy. Do not abuse it!" By then, Green was removing a bushel of broken bottles, cans, paper and other trash every other week. In his comments to a local reporter, he made a suggestion now common wisdom in many parks. "If you bring it on, take it off."[31] The photograph above was published with the *Messenger* article written at the time. (Granger Green is kneeling; Clifford Murphy, Sr. is standing.) (Photograph courtesy *Messenger Post* newspapers.)

In the 25 years after the state legislature proposed abandoning Squaw Island there were several attempts by the state to transfer jurisdiction, and maintenance costs, to local governments. In 1972 the Department of Environmental Conservation proposed leasing the island to Ontario County as a park. The interest of the Board of Supervisors was concisely summarized by a Messenger reporter who wrote that, "The suggestion was discussed briefly in a meeting... But supervisors were noncommittal." Later reports indicate that the Supervisors estimated the cost to restore the island would be $200,000. The "list of qualifications" presented by Department of Environmental Conservation was referred to the county Environmental Quality and Parks Committees. It certainly did not make the proposal attractive to the supervisors.[32] Within months, Supervisors' Board chairman, Herendeen, again brought up the question of Squaw Island being leased to the county. The proposal was referred to the Planning and County Buildings and

Environmental Quality Committees. However, the pending establishment of a Preserve Trust, keeping the island a state responsibility, was noted and no more was heard of the island leasing proposal.[33]

Several years later, J. W. Aldrich of the State Nature and Historical Preserve Trust proposed that the City of Canandaigua be given responsibility for maintaining the island after the state spent $10,500 on preservation.[34]

In 1974, the Ontario County Environmental Management Council estimated that the cost of reinforcing the island shoreline would be $31,000.[35] That recommendation was supported by a report to the Board of Supervisors from Clyde Maffin, County Historian. Acting on a recommendation of Clifford Murphy, Sr., Maffin proposed an inexpensive do-it-yourself reinforcement of the island. A group of SCUBA divers, and the local Army Reserve engineer unit, might be able to work on the island, Maffin said.[36] The widely divergent cost estimates for island work, and the seeming difficulty of the task, continued to discourage work on the island. Then Board Chairman, John Hicks, noted that the Pure Waters organization had "requested that the project be released to them," which had been done.[37]

In 1977, two years after the transfer of Squaw Island to the Department of Environmental Conservation, state crews, working for the State Nature and Historical Preserve Trust, began a month-long installation of cedar log cribbing around the perimeter of the island. The project was named in the Trust authorization bill, however no funding was included. The estimated cost of the project, variously stated as $9,500-$10,000, was paid from surplus funds in the DEC budget. The cribbing was reinforced with course crushed stone designed to protect the island for 20 years. The state crew had to build a special raft, floated on steel drums, to transport tools and materials to the island.[38]

# Squaw Island Preservation Society

A little over 20 years later, a group calling itself the Squaw Island Preservation Society was formed to save the island once again. The predicted 20-year life of the 1977 preservation work had obviously expired by 1998. Amid public outcry, the Department of Environmental Conservation proposed abandoning the island once again, or having the county take it over. The Daily Messenger denounced that proposal in an editorial.[39] Paul Hudson, Janis Barnes (daughter of Granger Green), Canandaigua Mayor, Ellen Polimeni, and 60 other members and friends of the Preservation Society met for the first time on January 9, 1999. By the time the project was completed, some 350 people had joined or assisted the society. Hudson, whose idea spawned the group, promoted its organization within the Ontario County Historical Society. That group agreed to do the bookkeeping and provide the benefit of its tax-exempt status. Financing was worked out with Canandaigua National Bank.

Taking their cue from an environmental study by SUNY Geneseo professor, Richard Young, Preservation Society members began to formulate a strategy to meet their goal. Within weeks they had convinced the State Department of Environmental Conservation, and several state legislators, to help them raise the money to preserve the island. The Society sold t-shirts, hats, and other memorabilia.

Delivering the "checks." Oct. 12, 2000. L-R: Stuart Norris, Clifford Murphy, Jr., Assemblyman Kolb, Paul Hudson, Earl Coleates, Janis Barnes (daughter of Granger Green), John Hicks (Regional Dir. DEC)

They also hosted programs with music and refreshments at the nearby Inn on the Lake. Ultimately the Squaw Island Preservation Society raised more than $30,000 for the project which quieted state objections to the project. The majority of the money needed ultimately came from state grants, "member items" in the state budget. $50,000 from the Environmental Bond Act, and a $20,000 appropriation sponsored by Assemblyman Brian Kolb, provided the rest of the needed funding. Former Ontario County Administrator, John Hicks, serving as regional director of the state DEC, was able to turn around what had been a negative attitude by that agency.[40]

With funding assured, contractors working under DEC supervision encircled the island with boulders weighing up to 1000 pounds to insure it against further erosion "for about 100 years." The project, which took about six weeks, was estimated to cost $135,000. When the new rock seawall was in place, Ontario County donated 30 cubic yards of topsoil for the island which had shrunk to an area 155 feet by 55 feet by 2001.[41]

Today, a bronze marker on City Pier, overlooking Squaw Island, reminds its readers of the significance of the island and the dedication of Clifford E. Murphy, Sr. and his "Squaw Island Committee." The marker was dedicated on October 28, 1984.[42] In every generation it seems there have been those who have enjoyed Squaw Island. Some have studied the island. Some have lobbied for it. Others have merely left us useful and picturesque descriptions, photographs or artistic interpretations. It is a legacy from the distant past. As Granger Green's sign still reminds visitors, it is an "Island to Enjoy."

Dedication of the Squaw Island marker on the city pier. The marker honors Clifford E. Murphy, Sr. who convinced the state to implement erosion-prevention measures. (Left to right): Mrs. Murphy; Clifford Murphy, Jr.; Leo Hosenfeld, chairman of the memorial committee. Courtesy Messenger Post Newspapers. Photograph by Bob Matson. *Daily Messenger.* Oct. 29, 1984 (p. 3).

Original island sign on Canandaigua city pier. Postcard circa 1950. Courtesy John Cuddeback.

Postcard view of the island dated 1909.

Postcard view of island at the turn of the 20th Century. Postmarked 1914. "Undivided" postcard back, however indicates publication prior to 1907.

State barge bringing equipment to the island. 1997. Photograph courtesy Paul Hudson.

Construction equipment on the island during the 1997 project. Photograph courtesy Paul Hudson.

Construction barge returning from a day of work on the island. Photograph 1997 courtesy Bonnie Yonker.

Raking down the topsoil as the preservation project is completed. Photograph 1997 courtesy Paul Hudson.

# John M. Clarke and the "Water Biscuits" of Squaw Island

Dr. John M. Clarke (1857-1925), a Canandaigua native, held several important positions at the New York State Museum. The son of Academy principal, Noah T. Clarke, he was also a nephew of Mary Clark Thompson. Mrs. Thompson supported many of Dr. Clarke's scientific endeavors as well as plans to beautify Canandaigua Lake and Squaw Island.

After attending Canandaigua Academy, Dr. Clarke entered Amherst College from which he received a Bachelor of Arts degree in 1877 at the age of 20. Amherst granted Clarke a Master of Arts degree in 1882. After teaching a year at Canandaigua Academy, Clarke joined the faculties at Amherst and Smith Colleges. His specialty was the study of Devonian rocks and fossils. Clark undertook doctoral studies at the university at Göttingen, Germany in 1883. He returned the following year without graduating and resumed teaching at Smith College as well as the Massachusetts State Agricultural College.

In 1886 John Clarke was named Assistant New York State Paleontologist, working with renowned science pioneer, James Hill. He continued in the service of the state for the rest of his life. He eventually served as Assistant State Geologist and Paleontologist (1893-1898); State Paleontologist (1898); and State Geologist and Paleontologist and Director of Science and the State Museum (1904-1925). Clarke also served as a part-time professor of geology at Rensselear Polytechnic Institute.

Clarke wrote more than 300 articles, pamphlets and studies, as well as seven books. Local studies included the Devonian fauna of Ontario County (1885) and the Naples fauna (1899, 1902). In 1904 Clarke, and Naples resident D. Dana Luther, published the stratigraphic and paleontologic map of Canandaigua and Naples quadrangles. Through Clarke's work with Luther, the "Naples Devonian Tree," discovered in Grimes Glen, became a featured specimen in the collection of the State Museum.

John Clarke's awards include the Hayden Memorial Geological Award (1908); the Spindiaroff Prize of the International Congress of Geologists at Stockholm (1910); and the gold medal of the Wild Life Permanent Protection Fund (1918) for his work protecting waterfowl in Gaspé, Canada. In 1925, he received the Thompson Gold Medal of the National Academy of Science. Clarke also received six honorary doctorates from the University of Marburg (Germany), Amherst College, Colgate University, Johns Hopkins University, the University of Chicago, and Princeton University.

Dr. Clarke is buried in Albany Rural Cemetery in the Capital District.

Clarke's study of "The Water Biscuit of Squaw Island…" was published in the *Bulletin of the New York State Museum*, v. 8, #39, October 1900. It is reprinted here so that readers of this booklet can better understand the scientific, as well as the historical importance of Squaw Island.

Postcard view from the west shore about the time John Clarke studied the island.

# THE WATER BISCUIT OF SQUAW ISLAND, CANANDAIGUA LAKE, N. Y.

BY JOHN M. CLARKE

(Plates 12-15)

Canandaigua lake is one of the well-known chain of Finger lakes in western New York which hang like pendants from below the south shore of Lake Ontario. This pretty sheet of water, about 14 miles long in its gently sinuous course, is a short section of an ancient waterway impounded by a dam of drift at its southern end. Near the lower or northern end of the lake, where its waters touch the village of Canandaigua, is its single island, a little spot of gravel and sand which the counter currents have piled up. Ever since Gen. Sullivan in 1779 carried firebrand and death among the Indians of this section, this bit of land has been known as Squaw island, and according to local tradition, here the women of the fighting braves took refuge from their burning villages. The adjoining sketch map shows the position of this island with reference to the shores of the lake. It will be seen that it lies west of the axis of the lake and opposite the *embouchure* of a little inlet. Its form is slightly elongated north and south, and from its northern end to the east side of the reedy cove, where the inlet comes in, a sand bar extends, along which at low water one can wade to the mainland. The inlet, which is known as Sucker brook, is a little stream which has grown smaller as the boys who played about it have grown to manhood. It heads in the northern part of the township of Canandaigua and in the upper reaches of its brief, meandering course of 8 or 10 miles it passes over a region of limestone and calcereous shales, cuts, kames and till piles where limestone boulders abound. In this way its waters have become well impregnated with lime. The north shores of Squaw island and the lake bottom about it and over its northward sand bar are covered with flat, whitish calcareous cakes of circular or oval shape, in size ranging from a dime to a half dollar. To pick up one of these, well dried on the surface of the island and break it in half, seems enough to convince the reflective mind at once of their nature and mode of formation. It often contains as a central nucleus a beach pebble of shale or limestone, a twig, or a bit of charcoal from some youngsters' camp fire. About this a white or greenish travertine has been deposited in concentric layers which show themselves with distinctness. Often the interior of the cake is soft and powdery. Frequently the cake shows an imperfect fibrous structure. There is little doubt that this calcareous matter is constantly supplied by the influx of the lime-charged waters of Sucker brook. The little island and its bar lie directly in the course of this stream and receive the charge of carbonate of lime before these waters have diffused themselves over the wider surface and through the greater depths of the lake to the south. It is only on the north side of Squaw island that this water biscuit is found in abundance, and there almost every pebble is a biscuit. This apparently simple mode of concentric deposition in the formation of these bodies is of itself sufficiently interesting for record, and it would not be easy for the writer to cite a parallel. Here is actually a coarse, uncemented oolite forming under peculiar but very simple conditions.

This however is not the whole story. On picking one of the water biscuits from the lake bottom its surface is found to be smooth, slimy and often greenish; exposure on the shore bleaches it white. The calc-carbonate being dissolved in dilute acid and entirely removed, there remains a soft, spongy, organic residuum of precisely the volume of the original biscuit. From within will drop out the nucleus, rupturing the side of the soft mass. On examination, this organic matter proves to be a felted mass of filaments of fresh-water algae, which have been examined for me by Prof. C. H. Peck, the state botanist, and one of the species identified as probably Isatjs fluviatilis. In the judgment of Prof. Peck there are several such species, and entangled among them are to be found diatoms, the whole so reproducing the form of the biscuit as to make it clear that the calcareous deposit has been permeated with the organic matter.

It is quite clear that the process of formation of these peculiar bodies has been the following. The beach shale and débris have become incrusted by a growth of algae, and the latter, stealing away for their requirements the excess of free carbon dioxid in the water necessary to keep the carbonate of lime in solution, have thus caused a precipitation of the lime salts. The process has been continuous, as when a new precipitation formed a concentric continuous deposit of lime carbonate, the new surface became coated with the algae and in consequence fresh precipitation followed. The whole forms a most interesting instance of the influence of plant growth on the formation of lime deposits.

A group of Squaw Island water biscuit.

It is appropriate to note in this connection that European authors have recorded the occurrence of similar spheric masses of filamentous algae in various fresh and brackish lakes. Some of these bodies from the lochs of the Hebrides have been described and illustrated by Barclay, who designates them as *algoid lake balls*.[1]

---

[1] G. W. W. Barclay, "On some algoid lake balls found in South Uist." Proceedings Royal soc. Edinburgh. 1886, 13: 845, pl. 30.

These masses are described as composed of "innumerable alga filaments so intertwined and matted together as to form an outer covering of almost felt-like consistency which could not however be torn open without difficulty. This outer coating varied from about $\frac{1}{30}$ to $\frac{2}{30}$ of an inch in thickness, and the interior of the balls consisted so far as the naked eye could see only of mud. . . A microscopic examination of the balls shows that they are composed of a filamentous alga, C l a d o p h o r a  g l o m e r a t a . . . The interior is seen to be filled with diatoms and the decomposing inner ends of the radiating filaments". Similar bodies, it is stated, come from Ellesmere in Shropshire and from the lakes of Sweden, Norway, northern Germany, Austria and upper Italy. These so called lake balls while organically similar to the water biscuit of Canandaigua lake, are entirely without calcareous deposit or inorganic nucleus. They would seem to be comparable to the condition of this water biscuit after the removal of the calcareous matter. While no explanation has been offered for the peculiar glomerated mode of growth of the alga, it may be that the noncalcareous lake balls have formed in waters without excessive content of lime carbonate. That the deposition of this lime carbonate in the formation of the water biscuit has gone on *pari passu* with the growth of the alga, as above suggested, seems quite clear.

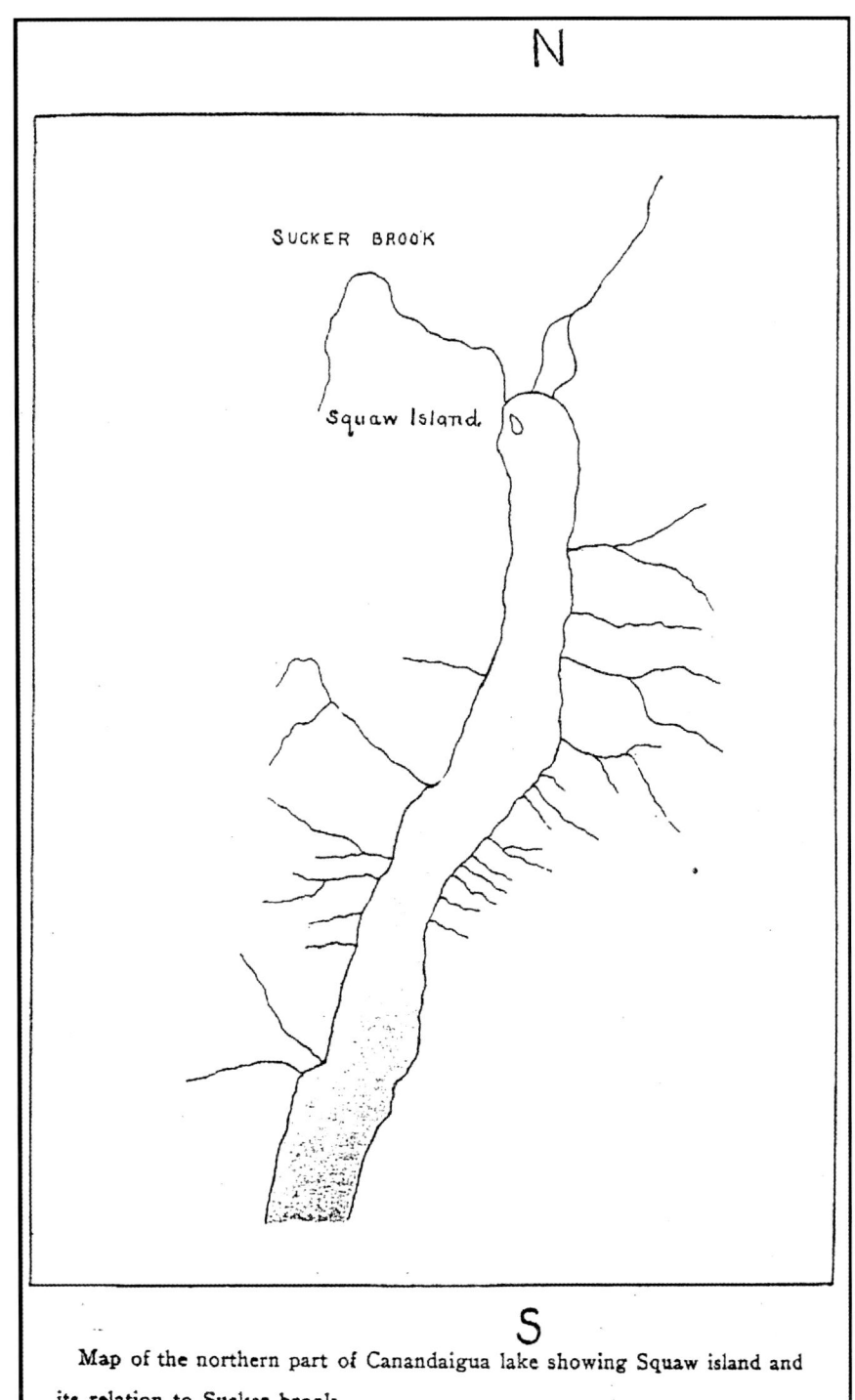

Map of the northern part of Canandaigua lake showing Squaw island and its relation to Sucker brook

# Charles T. Mitchell: Physician, Angler and Writer

Dr. Charles T. Mitchell, author of "A Romance of Squaw Island," was born in Hamilton, Ontario, Canada, January 30, 1836. The oldest of six children, his parents were Charles and Betsey E. (Drake) Mitchell. His father was a native of Madison County, NY. Betsey Drake was a resident of LeRoy, NY where she married the elder Charles Mitchell in 1834. Soon after their marriage, the Mitchells moved to Paris, Ontario, Canada where the younger Charles was reared.

Charles T. Mitchell entered Warsaw (NY) Academy at the age of 19 and remained there one year. Following that he worked in his uncle's hardware store making fanning mills for three years. At the end of that time the future doctor began the study of medicine in the office of Dr. S. W. Cooke of Paris, Ontario. In 1862 Charles T. Mitchell served in an army hospital in Washington, DC, returning to Canada and a course of study at Victoria College, now part of the University of Toronto. He graduated in 1863 and began a three-year practice of medicine in Ionia, Michigan. About 1866 Dr. Mitchell moved to Geneva, NY, where he worked at the Geneva Hygienic Institute on Pulteney Park. There he took an interest in the practice of Homeopathic Medicine. During the 1874-1875 school year, Dr. Mitchell attended the Homeopathic Hospital College in Cleveland, Ohio, graduating at the end of the term. He then relocated to Canandaigua, NY.

Dr. Mitchell and his wife were active in the First Congregational Church were he served as treasurer for many years. He was also an officer of the local Masonic lodge for three decades and an organizer of the Canandaigua Anglers Association. In keeping with Dr. Mitchell's interest in Squaw Island, he was a frequent writer of prose and poetry related to the lake and fishing. In 1900 Mitchell published a small volume of poetry, **Down the Outlet**. He was also an expert on sea and fresh water shells and was president of the Canandaigua Botanical Society. Charles T. Mitchell was also a charter member of the Homeopathic Medical Society of Ontario County (which once included Yates County, as well). He served as the Society president from 1880-1882. Later in life, Dr. Mitchell was also a member of the Canandaigua Microscopical Society.

Dr. Mitchell married Adellia Cooper of Waterloo, NY in 1865. Their one child, Florence G., died in 1878 at the age of 11. Adellia passed away in 1897. Dr. Mitchell, who died December 22, 1923, is buried with his wife and daughter in Woodlawn Cemetery.

Squaw Island, Canandaigua Lake

# A ROMANCE OF SQUAW ISLAND

Charles T. Mitchell, MD

To the people of my friendship,
To the lovers of my stories,
Dwelling in this new born city,
In the comfort of their homesteads,
On the shores of "Chosen Water,"
In their cabins by the lakeside,
As they gather 'round the lamplight,
Gather 'round the blazing camp-fire,
To recount the day's adventures,
Making plans for morrow's movements,
I would come again with greetings,
In these lines of rhythmic writing,
That I may once more contribute
To their pleasure and contentment.

**INSPIRATION**

In My years of old age idling,
When my time seems slowly drifting
With life's current, ever onward
To the bourne of the hereafter,
I can feel the spirit prompting
Still another song to sing them,
Still another story tell them,
Of the days that were, and are not,
Vanished in the flight of geese,
Stamped on geologic records,
Written on historic pages,
Told in tales of Indian legends.

**INVITATION**

You who love the fickle Springtime,
With its balmy air and bird songs;
Love the wild flowers, ferns and mosses,
Love the snowshoes and toboggan,
Find delight in mountain climbing,
Scenting all the woods with sweetness;
You who love the charming Summer,
With its clover blooms and honey;
Love the woodlands and the meadows,
Grateful in their shade and sunshine;
You who love the breath of Autumn,
From the orchards and the cornfields;
Love the smoky Indian Summer,
With its air of dreamy mildness;
You who love the blustering Winter,
With its ice-bound streams and snowfalls;
Sit in groups around the fireside,
Listen to this island romance.

## THE GLACIER

In the dim and misty ages,
Misty geologic ages,
Epoch known as Pleistocene,
When the earth had lost her balance
Through upheaval and subsidence,
Through the burden of great snowfalls,
Or by shifting of her axis,
Through some cosmic evolution,
From the regions of the North-Wind,
From the polar regions southward,
Came the ice-sheet slow advancing,
Came the great Laurentide glacier;
Covering all the earth with silence,
Crushing all of life beneath it,
Burying mastodon and mammoth,
Felling trees as they were pipe-stems.
Tropic regions changed to arctic,
Blocked were rivers in their flowing.
Mountains leveled by its grinding,
Strewed great boulders in its pathway,
Scooped out lakebeds as with shovels,
Unearthed fossils of past ages,
Left on rocks its signal markings,
Left moraines to tell the story,
Left its trail in all the valleys,
As it flowed in progress onward.
Ages multiplied by ages,
Saw this ice-sheet slow receding,
Melting by the heat of pressure,
Melting by the warmth of sun beams,
By the falling rain upon it,
By the breath of South-Wind on it,
To the regions of the North-Wind,
To the polar regions northward;
By its floodings and its drainings,
Cutting gorges through the limestone,
Tumbling over shelves of sandstone,
Opening runways for the rivers,
Leaving lakes in all the hollows.

## THE LAKE

Thus was formed "The Can-a-dar-que,"
Thus was born our "Chosen Water,"
Cradled in the lap of mountains,
Nursed by springs eternal flowing,
Rocked by breezes from the Southland,
Sparkling in the morning sunshine,
Placid in the heat of noonday,
Restless from the swell of midnight.
North and south the curving beach-lines,
East and west the wooded hillsides.
Current gently flowing northward,
Over bars and rocky ledges,
Over deep and shallow bottoms,
Ever through the Outlet seeking
A winding pathway to the sea.

## SQUAW ISLAND

Like a gem in crystal setting,
An oasis in the desert,
Where the shore-line curves to westward,
Joins the margin to the southward,
Sheltered by the arms of willows,
By the drooping limbs of elm trees,
Kissed by rippling waves at sunrise,
Smiling in the crimson sunset,
Casting shadows in the moonlight,
Chanting melodies by starlight,
On the breast of "Chosen Water"
Lies the babe of "Sleeping Beauty."
Clothed in Nature's garb of verdure,
Green in Springtime, brown in Autumn,
Bleak and lonely in the Winter,
When the north wind blows upon it.
Tall and stately trees adorn her,
Swaying gently in the west wind,
Reaching ever upward, skyward,
Catching all the gleams of sunlight,
Bathing in the summer showers,
Shading all the sandy margins,
By the downward drooping branches.

## THE FOREST

On the banks of "Chosen Water,"
All along the pebbly shore-lines,
Back upon the rugged hillsides,
On the bluffs and rocky headlands,
Grew the pine trees and the hemlocks,
Grew the birches, oaks and basswoods,
Blooming dogwoods and azaleas,
Climbing vines and tangled thickets;
Clothing all the land with forest,

Shading all the rippling streamlets,
As they dashed through glens and gorges,
Wakened by the voice of Springtime,
Freshened by the early raindrops,
As they fell in copious showers.
    Out beyond in open spaces,
Spread the meadows green and grassy,
Fragrant with the bloom of flowers,
When the South-Wind blows across them.
    In the thicket sprang the wild beast,
On the meadows fed the red deer,
On the outskirts native wood birds
Sang and nested in the branches.
    Down among the reeds and rushes,
In the low and swampy places,
Nesting wild fowl sought concealment,
Food and shelter for their younglings.
    When the sun at evening setting,
Rested on the western hilltops,
All the trees along the margins
Cast their shadows on the water.

## THE INDIANS

    At some prehistoric period,
Early in Creation's progress,
From a green and silent valley,
In the shadow of a mountain,
On the shore of Can-a-dar-que,
Sprang a tribe of Indian people,
Sprang the brave Nun-de-wa-o-no
At the call of the Great Sprirt.
    In the forests stood their wigwams,
Cabins built of bark and deer skins,
Grouped to form the tribal village,
Near the pleasant water-courses.
    Round the doorways played the children,
Taught to make their bows and arrows,
How to make their nets for fishing,
Learned the arts of war and hunting.
    On the moist and fertile meadows,
Down along the river borders,
Stood their orchards and their cornfields,
Ripening in the Autumn sunshine.
    In the gardens worked the women,
Where were growing beans and squashes,
Which, with wild-rice from the marshes,
Made their store of food for Winter.
    Hostile to the White-Man's coming,
On the warpath went the Red Men,
Went the young men, swift as runners,
Trained in all their sports and pastimes,
Some in feathers, some in warpaint,
With the tomahawk and scalp knife,
Terrorizing all the settlers,
Burning all their humble dwellings,
Taking men and women captive,
Desolating all the regions.

## THE INVASION

    This could be endured no longer.
So the "Father of the Nation,"
In his wisdom and discretion,
Sent an army of invasion,
Marched into the Indian country,
Burnt their wigwams, seized their horses,
Cut down all their bearing fruit trees,
Sacrificed their growing cornfields,
Devastated all their gardens,
Drove them from their favorite camp-grounds,
Scattered them beyond redemption.
    When they saw the White Man's footprints,
Saw the paleface warriors marching
With their weapons and their war train,
Fled they as were men affrighted,
Westward through the fens and marshes,
Left their wigwams and their cornfields,
At the mercy of invaders,
Waited for their foes in ambush,
In their hearts the thought of vengeance.
    In their flight with cautious movements,
In the darkness of the night-time,
When the moon shed not its brightness,
And the clouds obscured the starlight,
All the women and the children,
All the maidens who had lovers,
Found concealment on the Island,
Where they dwelt in watchful silence,
Till returning braves relieved them,
By their presence and protection.

## THE LOVERS

    Of the maidens who had lovers,
One alone, whose promise bade her
There await her warrior's coming,
Saw the last canoe departing,
Bade farewell to all her kindred,
Thinking only of her lover.
    When the evening twilight settled
Into darkness of the night-time,
Far across the moonlit waters,
Could be heard her plaintive singing:

"Come, my lover, I am waiting,
I will follow you, my husband."
  When the morning sun ascending,
Tinged the sky with rose and crimson,
Hands outstretched to Heaven imploring,
Prayed she for her lover's coming.
  Day by day she prayed and fasted,
Night on night she spent in singing,
Waiting for her lover's coming,
To redeem his pledge and promise.
  Far to westward in the forest,
As the camp-fire smoked and smouldered,
Weary, wounded and disheartened,
Thought he of his pledge and promise.
  With the fleetness of the roebuck,
With the silent tread of wild beast,
Like the noiseless flight of owlet,
Through the leafy woods he traveled;
Sped he as of one impassioned,
All his pathway through the forest;
On his face the damp of midnight,
In his heart the thought of maiden;
Heard the night-bird's solemn hooting,
Heard the sighing of the pine trees,
Felt the drooping boughs of hemlock,
As he swiftly passed beneath them.
  When the cool of morning brought him
To the reedy west lake margin,
He could see the lovely maiden,
With her outstretched arms imploring
That his coming might be hastened.
  At her lover's call she started,
Sprang to meet him in the water,
Sank into the miry bottom,
Sank beneath the trech'rous waters;
And before his swimming brought him
To the place of her departure,
She had passed the swinging portals
To the bourne of the hearafter.
  Quickly plunged he to the bottom,
Plunged beneath the bubbling surface,
From the weedy bottom raised her,
Bore her to the island margin,
Breathed upon her face and kissed her,
Praying that she yet might bless him
By her dark eyes opening widely.
  Thus he labored without ceasing,
Full of hope and yet of heart-break,
With no other thought impressing
Than return to life beholding.
  When the sun at eve descending
Saw no signs of life returning,
Mourned the warrior for his maiden,
Mourned he as of one forsaken,
Through the long and dreary night-time.
All night long he knelt beside her,
Speechless from the grief within him,
Till again the sun ascending
Through the portals of the morning,
Scattered all the gloom of darkness,
Painted all the sky with crimson.
  In the sand a grave he made her,
Softly lined with leaves and grasses;
Then with careful hands he raised her,
To his faithful breast he pressed her,
Laid her in the grave he made her;
Round her neck the pledge of wampum—
Covered her with leaves and grasses,
Heaped the clean white sand above her,
Marked the spot with branch of willow;
Water-lillies, white and fragrant,
Laid he on the mound above her,
To express the love he bore her.
  Then the little fire he kindled,
That her Spirit might be lighted
On its journey through the ether,
To the realms of the departed,
To the regions of the blessed.
  With a cry of pain and anguish,
Anguish as of one in sorrow,
Turned he slowly towards the mainland,
Walked with pensive mood to shoreward,
Disappeared within the forest.

**FINALE**

  You who read this island romance,
Read this tale of love and sadness,
In the quiet of your cabins,
By the shaded lamp of evening,
By the camp-fire's smould'ring embers;
Or who walk the beach by moonlight,
Paddle your canoe by starlight,
On the pleasant nights of summer,
Cease your laughing and your jesting,
Pause awhile and silent listen
To the strain of plaintive music,
Floating on the breath of evening.
'Tis the voice of Indian maiden,
Praying for her lover's coming.

      --Charles T. Mitchell

Reprinted from: *Ontario County Times*.
May 26, 1915.

# NOTES

[1] Hotra, Lynda McCurdy. *Landscape Artists of Canandaigua Lake 1830-1930.* Canandaigua, NY. Ontario County Historical Soc. 1981; Peacock-Jacobs, Anne. *Scenes of Monroe and Ontario Counties, Past and Present. Featuring Canandaigua Lake and Squaw Island.* Ontario County Historical Soc. 2003. Both publications reproduce several island paintings and provide short biographies of local artists.

[2] "Erase offensive place names." (Editorial) (Rochester, NY) *Democrat and Chronicle.* Jul. 1, 1997. p. 8-A. This editorial followed up on more general articles, published earlier, detailing Native American objections to the use of the term "squaw."

[3] Richards, Caroline Cowles. *Village Life in America.* Williamstown, MA. Corner House Pub. 1972. p. 134. The author quotes a letter to the editor of the *Ontario Repository,* Jun. 27, 1861. p. 2, which mentions Squaw Island by name, creating a romantic scene including "petrified Indians" at the foot of Bare Hill.

[4] "A Romance of Squaw Island." *Ontario County Times.* May 26, 1915. p. 3; Jul. 28, 1915. p. 8. The poem appears to be modeled on Longfellow's "Song of Hiawatha."

[5] For many years, a state highway marker proclaimed the site to be at the intersection of East Lake Road and old Routes 5 & 20. An archaeological dig, conducted by the Rochester Museum in the 1930's, pinpointed a pre-Iroquois site on the Sackett site on Arsenal Hill along old Routes 5 & 20 just past the city limits. No concrete evidence of the 1779 village has ever been identified. Sullivan's troopers recorded in their journals that the village was about a mile from the lake on high ground. The present site of Thompson Hospital would be about right, and in a line with the Sackett Site which may have been related.

[6] Yacci, Nancy H. *Images of America: Around Canandaigua.* Canandaigua, NY. Ontario County Historical Soc., 1996. p. 11. A photograph, from the OCHS collection, shows the rock in its original location.

[7] "Bronze Tablets on Swimming School and Squaw Island Boulders." *Ontario County Times.* Jul. 16, 1919. p. 7.

[8] There are several secondary accounts of the Sullivan-Clinton Expedition. Among the most comprehensive are Amory, Thomas C. *The Military Services and Public Life of Major-General John Sullivan, of the American Revolutionary Army.* (Port Washington, NY. Kennikat Press. 1968 (reprint 1868); Whittemore, Charles P. A General of the Revolution: *John Sullivan of New Hampshire* (New York. Columbia Univ. Press. 1961). Boardman, Fon W. Jr. Against the Iroquois: *The Sullivan Campaign of 1779 in New York State.* (New York. Henry Z. Walck. 1978) is really juvenile literature but comprehensive and readable; Graymont, Barbara. *The Iroquois in the American Revolution* (Syracuse, NY. Syracuse Univ. Press. 1972) contains an accurate and concise account of the expedition in Ch. VIII "Our Children Trembled." pp. 192-222.

[9] (Cook, Frederick, ed.) *Journals of the Military Expedition of Major General John Sullivan Against the Six Nations of Indians in 1779.* Glendale, NY. Benchmark Pub. Co. 1970. pp. 58, map enclosure #5.

[10] (Letter to the Editor.) "The Island." *Ontario County Journal.* Feb. 15, 1875. p. 3.

[11] (Letter to the Editor.) "The Island." *Ontario County Journal.* Feb. 15, 1875. p. 3.

[12] "—The authorities of this village..." *Ontario County Times.* May 11, 1881. p. 3.

[13] "—The lake continues..." *Ontario County Times.* Nov. 6, 1895. p. 3.

[14] "The level of the lake..." *Ontario County Journal.* Sep 15, 1899. p. 3.

[15] "The lake is low enough..." *Ontario County Journal.* Sep. 25, 1903. p. 3.

[16] "The lake level..." *Ontario County Journal.* Jan. 26, 1906. p. 3.

[17] "The Steamboat Launch." *Repository and Messenger.* Sep. 28, 1867. p. 4.

[18] "The dredging crew..." *Ontario Repository.* Oct. 22, 1903. p. 5.

[19] "Why not colonize..." *Ontario County Journal.* Sep. 25, 1903. p. 3. On Dec. 22, 1904, the *Ontario Repository-Messenger* (p. 5) printed an article with the headline, "Four Italians Shot. Wild Riot Last Night Among Sonnenberg Masons." It began with a statement that "a characteristic Italian riot occurred at the corner of Niagara and Pleasant-sts." The previous evening. It was typical of the anti-immigrant articles of the period. Perhaps more significant is the fact that the *Repository-Messenger* and the *Journal* usually represented opposing political views.

[20] Clarke, John M. "The Water Biscuit of Squaw Island, Canandaigua Lake, N.Y." Bulletin of the New York State Museum. Vol. 8. No. 39. Oct. 1900. pp. 195-198. Albany, NY. New York State Education Dept. 1900; Clarke, John M. (letter) "Squaw Island." *Ontario County Times.* Aug. 4, 1915. p. 2; "Squaw Island State Reservation." *Twenty-Fourth Annual Report of the American Scenic and Historic Preservation Society, 1919.* Albany, NY. J. B. Lyon Co. 1919; A.L. Bloom. Prof. Dept. of Geological Sciences. Cornell Univ. Letter to Stephen Pierce. Mar. 16, 1994 Brooks McKinney. Assoc. Prof. Dept. of Geoscience. Hobart and William Smith Colleges. Letter to Stephen Pierce. Mar. 17, 1994. "Historic Squaw Island Becomes State Property." *Ontario County Times.* Aug. 21, 1918. p. 1. State news releases from the early 1950s mention that Squaw Island was a "gift" to the state. There is no deed for the island and it undoubtedly became state land by virtue of being part of the lake bottom. The only "owners" who could have claimed otherwise were the heirs of Gideon Granger do did receive a deed to the lake bottom in 1817. Ontario Co. Land Records. Liber 29. pp. 349-350. The state Court of Appeals overturned that claim in 1931 *(Granger v. City of Canandaigua)*. It appears that Dr. Clarke merely got the island, already state property, a special designation. In 1981, journalist Charles Wilson reported that the Finger Lakes Parks Commission acquired the island Jul. 1, 1928 and transferred it to the State Education Department in 1944. See: Wilson, Charles. "Squaw Island—it's a world apart." (Rochester, NY) *Democrat and Chronicle.* Sep. 8, 1981. pp. 1-B, 2-B.

[21] Riding, Robert and Larisa Voronova. "Recent freshwater oscillatoriaacean analogue of the Lower Palaeozoic calcareous alga *Angulocellularia.*" *Lethaia: An international journal of palaeontology and stratigraphy.* Vol. 15. No. 2. 1982. pp. 105-114.; Dean, Walter E. and Thomas D. Fouch. "Lacustrine Environment." in Scholle, Peter A., et. al., (eds.) *Carbonate Depositional Environments.* Tulsa, OK. American Assn. of Petroleum Geologists, 1983. pp. 98-130.

[22] Young, Richard A. "Geologic Origin and Modification of Squaw Island, Canandaigua Lake." Dept. of Geological Sciences. SUNY Geneseo. Geneseo, NY. Dec. 9, 1998.

[23] Will of Mary Clark Thompson. Ontario County land records. Liber 331. pp. 11-17. 1924. A good summary of Mrs. Thompson's bequests and charities can be found in Hotra, Lynda Mc Curdy. *Mary Clark Thompson: Canandaigua's Magnificent Benefactress.* Canandaigua, NY. Ontario County Historical Soc. 1984. pp. 37. The State Museum acknowledged the part Mrs. Thompson played in protecting Squaw Island in an article in the 1918 report of its Director. ("The Scientific Reservations

Under Control of The Museum," p. 16)

[24] "Squaw Island Park." *Ontario Repository-Messenger*. Apr. 28, 1904. p. 4.

[25] "Boulder Monument for Squaw Island." *Ontario County Times*. Feb. 26, 1919. p. 1; "At Home and About." *Ontario County Times*. Mar. 5, 1919. p. 7.

[26] "At Home and About. The falling of two large elms…" *Ontario County Times*. May 3, 1911. p. 7.

[27] "Assigned to Parks Commission." *Ontario County Journal*. Jul. 20, 1928. p. 1.

[28] "Dike System Planned for Squaw Island." *Victor Herald*. Feb. 25, 1949. p. 4.

[29] "Legislature Urged to Sell Historic Canandaigua Island." *Daily Messenger*. Mar. 1, 1951. p. 3; "Around the Towns." (Rochester, NY) *Democrat and Chronicle*. (Late ed.) Apr. 7, 1952. p. 15; "State Forsakes Squaw Island After 34 Years." *Daily Messenger*. Apr. 8, 1952. p. 3. Indeed the state paid so little attention to the island that a 1994 letter from Carl C. Widmer to Preston Pierce, County Historian, revealed that the island file at the DEC office in Avon contained only three unattributed newspaper clippings, circa 1952.

[30] "U.S. Squaw Island Funds To Be Sought." *Daily Messenger*. Apr. 29, 1975. pp. 1, 3; "Committee Drops Squaw Island Plan. Daily Messenger. May 16, 1975. p. 1; "Historic Site For Squaw Isle?" *Daily Messenger*. May 7, 1975. p. 3.

[31] "Squaw Island Restoration is 1-Man Committee Project." *Daily Messenger*. Feb. 12, 1969. p. 3; "Friend of Squaw Island Praised by State Official." *Daily Messenger*. Mar. 9, 1978. p. 1; Szkotak, Steve. "Squaw Island Littering Is Growing from Picnic Visitors." *Daily Messenger*. Jul. 6, 1979. p.3.

[32] "Squaw Island Now Protected From Waves." *Ontario County Times*. Jul. 23, 1924. p. 1; Szkotak, Steve. "Squaw Island Littering Is Growing from Picnic Visitors." *Daily Messenger*. Jul 6, 1979. p. 3; O'Connor, Tom. "Plaque returns to island." *Daily Messenger*. Aug. 15, 1985. p. 3.

[33] "State Urges County To Take Over Park." *Daily Messenger*. Jun. 1, 1973. p. 1. Seneca Town Supervisor, John Hicks, Chairman of the Environmental Quality Committee said his committee discussed the matter "briefly." 25 years later Hicks would be the DEC officer working with the Squaw Island Preservation Society. Wilson, Charles. "Squaw Island—it's a world apart." (Rochester, NY) *Democrat and Chronicle*. Sep. 8, 1981. pp.1-B, 2-B; Ontario County. Board of Supervisors. Proceedings. Nov. 9, 1972. p. 290.

[34] Ontario County. Board of Supervisors. *Proceedings*. Feb. 8, 1973. p. 38.

[35] "Aid Sought For Squaw Island Job." *Daily Messenger*. Apr. 15, 1977. p. 3. The City of Canandaigua considered annexing the island if funding developed.

[36] Joseph H. Carver, Environmental Coordinator. Letter to John Hicks. Feb. 19, 1974.

[37] "Pleas to Save Squaw Island May Be Muted by Fiscal Reality." (Rochester, NY) *Times-Union*. (Greater Rochester Ed.) May 13, 1974. p. 1-B; "Squaw Island May Erode Completely Away, Board Told." *Daily Messenger*. May 13, 1974. p. 3; "Voice of Reader. Let's Do It!" *Daily Messenger*. May 16, 1974. p. 4.

[38] Ontario County. Board of Supervisors. *Proceedings*. May 9, 1974. p. 126.

[39] Wilson, Charles. "Squaw Island—it's a world apart." (Rochester, NY) *Democrat and Chronicle*. Sep. 8,

1981. pp. 1-B, 2-B; "Squaw Island Park's Preservation Begun." *Daily Messenger.* Oct. 25, 1977. p. 1.

[40] "Squaw Island's fate debated." *Daily Messenger.* Oct. 11, 1998. pp. 1-A, 6-A; "Squaw Island fate on table." *Daily Messenger.* Oct. 29, 1998. p. 1-A; (Editorial) "State shouldn't dump Squaw Island." *Daily Messenger.* p. 2-E; Ontario County. Board of Supervisors. *Proceedings.* Dec. 13, 1999. pp. 3, 39. The Board of Supervisors simply referred the proposal to their Planning and Research Committee and took no further action. They did the same with the correspondence from Paul Hudson, leader of the Squaw Island Preservation Society.

[41] Mahoney, Bryan. "Squaw Island gets $70,000 grant." *Daily Messenger.* Oct. 13, 2000. p. 1-B, 2-B; Jones, Jack. "State grant lifts hope to save tiny local island." *Democrat and Chronicle.* Oct. 13, 2000. p. 3-B; Mahoney, Bryan. "Squaw Island to erode no more." *Daily Messenger.* Feb. 15, 2001. p. 1

[42] Robinson, Bill. "Group gathers to help save Squaw Island." *Daily Messenger.* Jan. 10, 1999. p. 1-B; "Squaw Island strategy emerges." *Daily Messenger.* Jan. 29, 1999. p. 1; Mahoney, Bryan. "Squaw Island project finished." *Daily Messenger.* May 31, 2001. p. 1-A, 7-A.

[43] Matson, Bob. "Clifford E. Murphy Sr. honored for work to save Squaw Island." *Daily Messenger.* Oct. 29, 1984. p. 3.

[44] This essay is based upon a longer, as yet unpublished, biographical essay, "Built on the Rocks of Ages: The Life and Work of John Mason Clarke," written by the author. A preliminary version was published in "The Historians' Newsletter of Ontario County," XV. January. 1998. pp. 7-13.

[45] Conover, George S. *History of Ontario County, New York.* Syracuse, NY. D. Mason and Co. 1893. Main Sec. pp. 186-187, 192. Family Hist. Sec. pp. 117-118; Ontario County. Surrogate Court records. Will of Charles T. Mitchell. Probated 1924; "Useful Career is Ended in Death." *Ontario County Journal.* Dec. 28, 1923. p. 1; "Dr. Charles T. Mitchell Died on Saturday A.M." *Ontario County Times.* Dec. 26, 1923. p. 1.

Front cover photograph by Janis Barnes